Great Scientific
Questions and the
Scientists Who
Answered Them™

HOW DO WE KNOW

THE NATURE

OF TIME

JOSEPHA SHERMAN

Great Scientific
Questions and the
Scientists Who
Answered Them™

HOW DO WE KNOW
THE NATURE
OF TIME

THE ROSEN PUBLISHING GROUP, INC.
NEW YORK

Published in 2005 by The Rosen Publishing Group, Inc.
29 East 21st Street, New York, NY 10010

Library of Congress Cataloging-in-Publication Data

Sherman, Josepha.
How do we know the nature of time/Josepha Sherman.—1st ed.
    p. cm.—(Great scientific questions and the scientists who
          answered them)
Summary: Explores mankind's developing notion of time, from the first primitive clocks and sundials to the expanding space-time of the theory of relativity.
Includes bibliographical references and index.
ISBN 1-4042-0073-8 (library binding)
1. Time—Juvenile literature. [1. Time.]
I. Title. II. Series.
QB209.5.S47 2004
115—dc22

                                 2003015578

Manufactured in the United States of America

Cover: Quartz clocks
Cover inset: A sundial

Contents

Time in the Ancient World

What is time? It cannot be seen or touched. Yet it seems to exist, or no one would age or even be born, and there wouldn't be seasons or even any day and night. But we're not so sure about what the word "time" actually means, and we use the word in many ways to mean many related things. For instance, if someone is bored, we

may say that he "has time on his hands." If someone else really likes a novel, we may say that she reads it "time after time."

Adding to the confusion, the word "time" can mean different things to different people. It can mean the force that keeps events going in what seems to be an unvarying stream from the past through the present and on to the future. It can also mean a passage between events, or a specific number of minutes, hours, days, and so on. In fact, not everybody has even ever agreed on how time does operate. Some cultures, including our own North American and European ones, believe in "linear time." That is, we see time as a river, something that keeps steadily flowing from point A down to point Z, without ever going from point Z

Ctesibius is credited with inventing the water clock around 250 BC. He is known as the Edison of the Alexandrian School. The water clock was often used to measure the length of speeches in the courtroom.

back "upstream" again. Other cultures, such as those influenced by Buddhism and Hinduism, see time as cyclical. Everything that once happened will happen again. In Hindu belief, creation is cyclical and never ending. Each cycle has four great yugas, or epochs of time: Satya yuga, Treta yuga, Dwapar yuga, and Kali yuga, lasting from four thousand years to one thousand years, respectively. Time and creation then "begin to end and end to begin."

Whatever time may actually be, it seems likely that for as far back as human beings have been aware, people have realized that there were such things as time and the passage of time. They could see that the seasons changed and plants grew and that people and animals went from babies to adults and then died. The

Al-Razzaz al-Jazari, a mechanical engineering genius of the twelfth century, was born in the area between the Tigris and Euphrates rivers in Iraq. At right is his detailed depiction of a water clock. The repetitive motion of the dancing figurines, or automata, helped keep time.

الحَامَات بالضَّوْ وَهَذِهِ صُوْرَةٌ مَا وَصَفْتَهُ وَاضِحَةٌ

earliest measurements of time would have likely been the most obvious: the way that the sun, the moon, and the stars and planets seem to move across the sky. One of the obvious measurements would surely have been a solar year, which is the time that it takes for the earth to revolve around the sun. In addition, the changing shape of the moon would also have given human observers an easy way to keep track of time. The moon waxes and wanes on a regular schedule, from new moon (completely dark) to first quarter (half moon) to full moon and back again every 29.5 days, the division that would eventually be called a month.

It would have been important for those early humans to know the length of the days and the changing of the seasons. They would have had to know when the animals they needed to hunt for food would migrate or have their offspring. They would also have had to know when the plants they ate would bear seeds or fruit.

Early humans, living about 30,000 years ago, were nomadic, following the herds or looking for a new place to live. Since they traveled on foot, whatever they carried would have had to be lightweight. This would include any way to keep track of time. Carved bones found in Europe and Asia that have been dated as 30,000 years old may have been early forms of pocket calendars. These carvings seem to have been worked deliberately to show a lunar month—a month based on the time it takes for the moon to go through a cycle of waxing and waning. They are the perfect size for a human to easily carry or wear.

But as time passed, more settled and complex civilizations began to develop. City-states with large populations dependent on organized agriculture appeared. Knowing the time became more important to people, since they had to plan the planting and harvesting of their food supplies. Not only were years and months used for measuring time, but more specific points in the year were noted: the two major solstices, summer and winter, and two equinoxes, vernal (spring) and autumnal.

The summer solstice occurs near June 21 on our modern calendar. It is the time when the sun is at its northernmost point in our sky. This is the longest day of

the year. The winter solstice occurs near December 21, when the sun reaches its southernmost point in our sky. This is the shortest day of the year. In the Northern Hemisphere, the vernal, or spring, equinox occurs near March 20, when the sun passes the equator from south to north. On the vernal equinox, day and night are approximately the same length. The autumnal equinox occurs around September 22, when the sun passes the equator from north to south. Once again, as with the vernal equinox, day and night are approximately the same length.

THE FIRST RECORDS OF TIMEKEEPING

Around 3000 BC, in the civilization of ancient Sumer in Mesopotamia—in what is now Iraq—the Sumerians created a twelve-month calendar. Their months were based on lunar phases. They also divided the year into two seasons. The dry season was called *emesh*. It began around February or March. The wet season, *enten*,

Besides the calendar, the Sumerians invented the system of writing—cuneiform—which was first used for financial transactions.

began in September or October, with the arrival of the rains.

At about the same time, the civilization of the ancient Egyptians was growing along the Nile River. Although Egypt is mostly a desert land, every year the Nile flooded, bringing fertile mud onto the fields and making good harvests possible. Around 3000 BC, Egyptian astronomers noted that the first rising of the star Sirius in the morning sky marked the time that the Nile's flooding usually began. By about 1100 BC, they had created a catalog of what they could see of the universe with the naked eye. It included a list of star groups known as *decans*. The decans were useful for

keeping track of time: each star's rising at night marked the start of the next hour. Several wooden sarcophagi, or coffins, from about 2000 BC show diagrams that may have been solar clocks tracking the decans to tell time at night. Some of the Egyptian tombs from about 1400 BC have painted ceilings that not only provide a chart of the decans but of the lunar months as well.

Working with the information they had about the movements of the heavens and the lengths of the days, Egyptian astronomers devised a calendar of 365 days, with twelve months. Each month was made up of thirty days. Since the actual year doesn't divide evenly, there was extra time left over in the Egyptian calendar once every four years, the way there is with our modern leap year. They had three seasons: *ache*, or flooding, *proje*, or winter, and *schomu*, or summer.

The water clock measured time by the flow of water through a small tube. The hours were marked on the sides of the bowl that received the water. The floating rack (F) moved the pointer (G) at a steady rate.

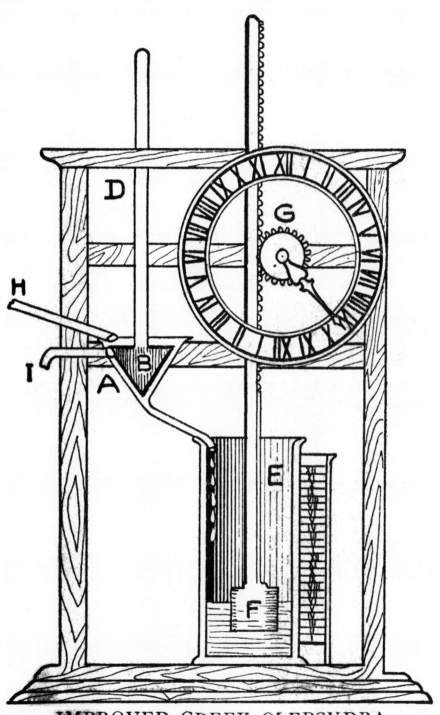

IMPROVED GREEK CLEPSYDRA

The Egyptians also kept track of time with sundials and water clocks. Sundials are circles marked at regular points with a raised marker. As the sunlight travels over the clock, the shadow created by the marker points to the time. Water clocks don't rely on sunlight. A water clock measures time by the regulated dropping of water from one bowl to another or from one bowl out onto the ground. Both sundials and water clocks date to about 1500 BC. The idea that the ancient Egyptians considered keeping time important can be assumed from the fact that a water clock was found in the tomb of Pharaoh Amenhotep I, who died around 1500 BC.

HOW THE GREEKS KEPT TIME

The next major civilization to make use of water clocks was that of ancient Greece. The Greeks started using water clocks around the fourth century BC and dubbed the devices clepsydras, or "water thieves," since the water was "stolen" from the bowls. Greek clepsydras were usually made of stone or metal, and they usually had sloping sides. Each water clock had a small hole at the bottom, out of which water could drip (or be "stolen" by gravity) at a nearly constant rate. Markings on the insides of the bowls showed the passing of time as the water level fell.

The Greeks also designed different styles of sundials, looking for more accurate ways to tell time. In addition to the standard flat sundial, there was also the hemicycle, which was shaped like half a bowl. In fact, by about 30 BC, there were at least thirteen different styles of sundial being used throughout Greece and Italy.

The Greeks used the motion of the stars in timekeeping as well. Proof of this comes in the *Works and Days* of Hesiod, an early Greek poet who lived and wrote around 700 BC. He gives farmers information about the times for plowing and harvesting, writing that "when the Pleiades [a cluster of stars in the constellation Taurus] rise it is time to use the sickle, but the plough when they are setting" and

when the star Arcturus can be seen at dawn, it is time to pick grapes.

The Greek calendar was a lunar one, and that eventually led to problems when the Greeks tried to link it to solar time. By 600 BC, an early calendar of twelve months of thirty days each had failed and been replaced by one with six thirty-day "full" months and six twenty-nine-day "empty" months. But that one failed as well. The Greek statesman Solon, who lived in the sixth century BC, also tried his hand at creating an improved calendar. He, too, failed. The Greek astronomer Meton invented yet another calendar, this time in 432 BC, but his doesn't seem to have been put into public use. Meton and another astronomer, Euctemon, are known for their invention of the *parapegma,* a stone tablet with pegs that could be moved to match the movement of the stars with special dates. Parapegmai were also made out of papyrus, a type of reed paper from Egypt that was used before the invention of wood pulp paper. By the end of the first century BC and into the first century AD, both the Greeks and the Romans began developing more elaborate, mechanized water clocks. The designers of these more modern devices were trying to make the flow of the water more constant by regulating the water pressure. But the new designs also put on quite a show for the viewer. Some water clocks rang bells or struck gongs. Others opened tiny windows to show little figures of people. Still others moved pointers or even featured models of the universe as the ancients understood it.

The most exotic of these mechanical water clock devices had to have been the eight-sided Horologion, also known as the Tower of the Winds. A Macedonian astronomer, Andronikos, erected the Horologion in the Athenian marketplace in the first century BC. The Horologion had a twenty-four-hour mechanized clepsydra, eight sundials (one on each of its eight sides), pointers for the eight winds—which gave the tower its name—and indicators of the seasons of the year and important astronomical dates and periods.

THE ROMAN CALENDAR

For all these exotic and not quite accurate ways of counting the hours, counting the days and years had become a true problem for the Romans. Their calendars were confusing and inaccurate. They

After consulting revered astronomers of the day, Julius Caesar instituted the Julian calendar on January 1, 45 BC.

counted the beginning of the month from the first sighting of the moon's crescent after the new moon. But they counted the year with a solar calendar. This meant that every four years, there were too many days. By 46 BC, the Roman calendar was off by about three months.

This lack of accuracy was definitely not good enough for the Roman dictator, Julius Caesar. He commissioned Sosigenes, an astronomer from Alexandria, Egypt, to design a calendar that was both more accurate and simpler to use. Sosigenes did his calculations and came up with a year having a length of 365.25 days. He divided this figure into twelve months and gave the months thirty or thirty-one days apiece. This left the problem of the leap year, the "extra" time that doesn't fit into the regular scheme. This extra time seems to have been a little too much for Sosigenes, who miscalculated it as being necessary every third year instead of every fourth year. As a result, inaccuracies were bound to creep into his calendar, even though Augustus Caesar, who followed Julius, saw to it that the leap year was calculated every four years. By this point, the new calendar worked very well, especially compared to what had come before. What Sosigenes had devised is known as the Julian calendar, after the man who commissioned it. The Julian calendar remained in use for centuries, and it is still used by

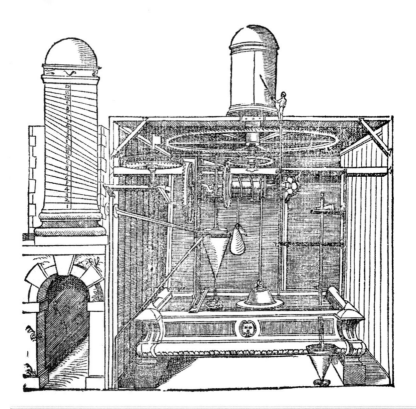

When the water clock was introduced in Rome, it was guarded by a civic officer, who ceremoniously filled it at stated times. The town's nobility and wealthy citizens would send servants to find out the exact time.

some of the Orthodox Christian churches around the world for the setting of feast days.

TIME IN THE FAR EAST

In the Far East, people were just as concerned as everyone else about finding the best way to keep track of time.

TIME IN THE ANCIENT WORLD

From about AD 200 on, the Chinese devised water clocks that powered various astronomical machines. Su Sung, a Chinese designer, was commissioned to build the most exotic of these in AD 1086. His machine included a clock tower that was over 30 feet (9.1 meters) tall, a continually revolving globe, and moving figurines that struck gongs.

The Chinese calendar was much more complicated. In China, the calendar was considered a sacred link between heaven and the ruling emperor. A special bureau of astronomy was in charge of the maintenance of the calendar. When a new ruler came to the throne, a new era began, with the year count starting from day one of the new reign. But an emperor could also declare the start of a new era after a natural disaster or a solar eclipse.

The earliest Chinese calendars of which we have records date to the Shang dynasty of the fourteenth century BC. They had two different forms of monthly cycles, one using a lunar system and the other using a solar one. The year was divided into twenty-four segments. The new year was originally marked at the time of the new

moon nearest the winter solstice, but a calendar reform in the second century BC set the calendar so that the winter solstice happened during the eleventh month. There were still problems, though, in matching up the solar and lunar calendars, and those remained unsolved until modern times.

RECORDING TIME IN THE NEW WORLD

In the New World, the Maya of Central America built a civilization that lasted from about 2600 BC to AD 900. The Maya had a strong interest in astronomy, as it was tied to timekeeping, the rhythms of agriculture, and religion. Without the technology or materials with which to build telescopes, they were forced to rely on their eyes. But they built sophisticated observatories and made use of shadow-casting devices, such as straight sticks, to let them trace the path of the sun. Rituals were carried out to ensure that the predictable cycling of the sky would continue.

The Maya used not just the sun and moon but also the planet Venus in designing a complex calendar. The Mayan year consisted of 360 days and each day had a name. The glyph (symbol) *kin* meant one day. *Winal* was a collection of twenty days, or a month. *Tun* was the glyph for a year, and *k'atun* was a time period of twenty years of 360 days each. A *baktun* was an epoch of 400 years.

The Aztec culture of Mexico, centered in what is now Mexico City, lasted from about AD 900 to 1517, when it was ended violently by the Spanish invasion from Europe. The Aztecs had a calendar as complex as that of the Maya. An Aztec year was made up of eighteen months and added up to 360 days. The five extra days were called *nemontemi*. They were thought to be unlucky and were days of sacrifice—often human. The Aztecs created enormous calendar stones carved in intricate relief. These stones seem to have served them both as ritual calendars and sundials. Whether or not the Aztecs thought of time as linear—flowing in

This 25-ton (23-tonne) Aztec calendar has a diameter of nearly 12 feet (3.7 m) and is 3 feet (0.9 m) thick. It was first discovered in 1760, buried under the main square of Mexico City. Tonatiuh, the Aztec sun god, is in the center.

a straight line—or circular isn't clear. There is some evidence for both ideas. It is known, though, that the Aztecs did give specific values to every day, year, and collection of years. They believed that the entire intricate passage of time needed specially timed offerings or sacrifices—plants, animals, or humans—if it was all to keep operating properly.

In South America, a people known as the Inca took over most of the western half of the continent, along the Andes mountain range. The Inca Empire lasted from 1438 until 1536, when, like the empire of the Aztecs, it was conquered by Spanish invaders. The Incan calendar, like that of the Maya, was based on the movements of the sun, the moon, and the stars. There is little information about the details of the calendar, although there were apparently twelve months tied into the agricultural cycle. The Inca also organized their work using six weeks of nine days each.

Lunar calendars are still in use in the world today, though usually not as the main way of keeping track of time. The modern Jewish calendar, for instance, is a lunar one, and as a result, Jewish holidays fall on different days of the common calendar each year. Some Islamic countries, such as Saudi Arabia, use a lunar calendar as well.

Mechanical Time

2

During the European Middle Ages, from about AD 500 to 1500, when the Renaissance began, there seems to have been little pressure for any major improvement in the measurement of time. Until around 1500, in fact, ordinary people didn't need to know the time, except in the most general way. They used the position of the sun, moon, and stars to tell them when, for example, it was midday or when it was midsummer. They simply didn't worry about time other than to determine the right season for planting or harvesting or knowing when a festival day might occur. The lives of most peasants were the same year after year, as would be the lives of their children and grandchildren. Time as a measure of change and progress was not a meaningful concept.

THE RELIGIOUS IMPORTANCE OF TRACKING TIME

The Catholic Church, however, was more concerned with time. Its scholars were busy working out the time of biblical events such as the Creation, and they were also concerned about Judgment Day, when the world as they knew it was supposed to end. Before the fifth century AD, the common belief in western Europe was that the world would only exist for 6,000 years, and this led to a great interest in what things would be like afterward. This interest lasted up through the end of the first millennium AD. In AD 1000, in fact, many people did

think that the end of the world had come and waited on hilltops all night for the Lord's final judgment. They had interpreted various events at the time as the fulfilling of the prophecy of Christ's return, including the fall of the Holy Roman Empire. When, instead, the sun rose as usual on the next morning, they must have felt sheepish, relieved, or both as they returned to their homes and work. But they weren't the only ones to be fooled like this. Some people at the end of the nineteenth century also believed that time had run out. They also went up onto hilltops to pray and wait for the end of the world all night and then went home, happy or disappointed, when sunrise came as usual.

No one is sure when the first mechanical clock was invented. One possible inventor may have been Pacificus, the archdeacon of Verona, who was born about 776 and died about 844. He was known to be a learned scholar and an astronomer as well as a churchman. Pacificus is said to have built some type of clock in the early ninth century, but not much else is known about it or what happened to it.

Above is a depiction of the coronation of Holy Roman Emperor Otto III. Otto befriended Pope Sylvester II, who is credited with the invention of the mechanical clock. The young emperor hoped to use the pope's knowledge of Arabic astronomy and Egyptian mathematics to rejuvenate the Roman Empire.

Another candidate for creator of the first mechanical clock is Pope Sylvester II, who was originally a monk named Gerbert. Born around 940 or 950, the pope was a highly educated scholar, skilled in several fields. In fact, people often whispered about him because of his learning, claiming that anyone that wise had to be a magician or even in league with the devil. Nothing

came of those odd whispers, and the pope is often credited with the invention of a mechanical clock around AD 996. But again, as with the story about Pacificus, there is no real proof of this. Pope Sylvester II died on May 12, 1003, without leaving any writing about clocks.

There is more tangible evidence of clock-making skills from the end of the thirteenth century. A clock was installed in St. Paul's Cathedral in London in 1286. The most entertaining part of the clock was the mechanical figures that struck a bell on the hour. Another clock was placed in a tower at Westminster Hall, London, in 1288. A third clock was added to Canterbury Cathedral in 1292.

Such clocks, though, were very rare, since they were large and expensive. They were also not very accurate. That didn't matter, though; ordinary people of the

After the Great Fire of London in 1666, St. Paul's Cathedral in London, England, was redesigned by Christopher Wren. It is considered to be his last great masterpiece. London's first mechanical clock was in the structure's west front.

thirteenth century still weren't worrying very much
about the concepts of past or future. They simply reck-
oned time by major events, like the crowning of a new
king or the time of a great storm. After all, it wasn't necessary for someone to know the specific hour if he or she
worked on a farm. The times necessary for peasants—
knowing when to plant and when to harvest—could be
learned from the changing seasons.

TIMEKEEPING: AN ECONOMIC NECESSITY

By the fourteenth century, as more and more people
moved into cities, and trade and craftsmanship
became the occupations of the townspeople, merely
glancing at a sundial or saying, "It happened on the
first day of King Stephen's reign," was no longer
enough. A middle class of merchants and small-scale
manufacturers appeared, and these people employed
many others in workshops and home handicraft pro-
duction. Manufacturers had to measure the value of
time spent producing goods. Merchants and bankers

needed to measure accurately the duration of loans, the interest earned on them over time, and how long it would take to ship goods from one port to another. Increasingly, people needed to know more precisely what time it was, and they needed to divide their day into specific hours. And as the methods of science began to become more widely accepted, there was a greater need for more precise measurement of time in experiments.

This need for more detailed ways to tell time marks the beginning of the true age of mechanical clocks. The first of these more modern clocks appeared during the first half of the fourteenth century, and they were installed in the towers of Italian cities. These clocks were fairly simple devices, driven by weight or, more specifically, gravity. They were relatively accurate due to what is called a verge-and-foliot escapement.

The verge of such a clock is a central vertical shaft within the body of the clock. The foliot is a freely swinging horizontal bar attached to it. The escapement is the wheel in a clock that keeps the pendulum moving by

allowing a tooth of cogged wheel to "escape" with each move. A pendulum is anything that is suspended from a fixed support so that it constantly oscillates, or swings freely back and forth, under the influence of gravity. Also within the body of such a clock is a horizontal spindle with a cord wrapped around it. A weight hangs from the cord. As gravity slowly pulls the weight down, the cord unwinds, turning the spindle. A gear on the spindle makes the escapement and the verge and foliot vibrate. At the same time, the escapement regulates the rate at which the spindle turns. The turning of the spindle moves a hand around the face of the clock.

An odd side effect of the coming of mechanical clocks was the separation of clock time from solar and lunar time. For the first time, people were looking to a machine to measure time, rather than consulting the

Here, an illustration of a timekeeping system is depicted by al-Jazari, in his Book of Knowledge of Mechanical Processes. *The studies and written works of thirteenth-century Muslim scholars helped preserve knowledge that otherwise would have been lost to the modern world.*

ت الغلبانا ب بكبر بصو
مق بده بحي بحي له مع بحي قبض
قص
هقل ابطابط ظ السلا لحفو بركا
ع كتبا النهر من با بض طبا بقض
ل ع عبى ا ا لجمد بك ت ا تحبح وقض
لبا ك للعا ن الجا لبحاول وقض فن ل
ن بح بح بحي بربى فوحبر بح بح بخ
كبا عاهم للعا ل البحد لط المفابا منه
سقتا ل المال بح ل فى بح بخ ط ل الد
ل لالتخ ى بح بم قض شتل بول ه
عبشا ل

position of the sun. Using mechanical clocks to measure time was very different from using natural events such as the sunrise or the vernal equinox. The movements of celestial bodies are subject to all sorts of real or apparent irregularities, depending upon long-term changes in the movements of the earth or the location of the observer on its surface. Now mechanical clocks imposed an inflexible regularity on time, abstracting it from the motion of the universe.

These clocks were still only relatively accurate, since there was no way to perfectly control the vibration of the escapement. Despite their lack of accuracy, though, clocks of the fourteenth century were often elaborate affairs. In 1352, a clock was placed in the cathedral of Strasbourg, Germany, that was truly amazing. It showed the current positions of the sun, moon, and other heavenly bodies in addition to the time of day. The clock had elaborate mechanical figures that included the twelve apostles, a crowing cock, a revolving celestial globe, and an automatic calendar dial.

THE PROBLEM OF TIME IN DISTANT LANDS

Until the fifteenth century, almost everyone lived by local time. It's easy to think like this: "Noon exists only for me and the people around me." But after the first successful voyage of Christopher Columbus in 1492, people were forced to realize that the world was too large for only local time to apply. "Noon" happened at different times in different places around the world.

The Portuguese mapmaker Pedro Reinel was the first to puzzle out a solution to the problem of time and navigation over distance. He simply broke up the distance into segments of local time. In 1506, he became the first person to draw a latitude scale on a prime meridian, an arbitrary north-south line that divided up time and space over the globe and the sky. Latitude lines run east to west and divide the globe into horizontal segments. But the Portuguese mapmakers knew that they needed to establish longitude as well. Longitude lines run north to south, and they are the

important dividers of local time. By the 1520s, the Portuguese knew that only a truly accurate clock would be able to solve the problem of accurately measuring longitude. There was no such clock yet.

THE SIXTEENTH CENTURY

The next great advance in clock design came in the sixteenth century from Peter Henlein of Nuremberg, Germany. Born in 1485, he became a master locksmith in 1509. Although very little is known about his life and career, he eventually invented the spring-powered clock. Unlike the verge-and-foliot clocks, which were generally very large, the spring clocks could be of any size. Getting rid of those bulky, heavy escapements and spindles meant that smaller clocks and even pocket watches could now be built. The wealthy eagerly bought these smaller clocks, delighted to have a timepiece that could actually be kept on a table or mantle. Henlein died a wealthy man in 1542. But there still wasn't a truly accurate clock.

A discussion about reforming the calendar took place under Pope Gregory XIII on October 15, 1582, by the Gregorian calendar council. The Gregorian calendar was not fully adopted by England or the American colonies until 1752.

Forty years later, in 1582, there was an improvement to the Western calendar as well. Pope Gregory XIII commissioned an improved version. This time, the problems surrounding the creation and proper placement of the leap year were solved. This corrected calendar was named after the pope who'd commissioned it, and it became known as the Gregorian

calendar. The Gregorian calendar is still in use in the Western world today.

A PRECISE BIRTH DATE OF THE EARTH?

However, even though the calendar had been corrected, most people around the world still had no idea of geological time, the vast spans of time necessary for the earth to take its present form and for living organisms to evolve. Most people still believed that the earth was only a few thousand years old. Fossils were thought to be the remains of creatures killed in the flood mentioned in the Bible, and this was not thought to have occurred all that long ago. Archbishop James Ussher of Ireland, who was born in 1581, added up the generations descended from Adam as described in the Old Testament and calculated the age of the earth from that. He wrote in his *Annales Veteris et Novi Testamenti*, published in 1654, that the earth had been created in 4004 BC. In fact, he stated specifically that the moment of creation had taken place on October 26, 4004 BC, at 9:00 AM. Ussher died in 1656,

but his chronology continued to be accepted, at least in western Europe, until the nineteenth century.

THE SEVENTEENTH CENTURY

Galileo calculated that the time of the pendulum's swing is not directly proportional to the pendulum's length but that the time squared is.

In 1602, the famous Italian scientist Galileo Galilei, who was born in 1564, turned his attention to a theory of motion. In 1604, he noted that a pendulum took just as long to make a wide arc as it did to swing through a small arc, and he saw the possibility of using pendulum theory to make a better clock. But he died on January 8, 1642, without having ever designed such a clock or even having published his work on pendulums.

A few years after Galileo's death, Dutch astronomer and mathematician Christian Huygens, who was born in 1629, began working on the physics of pendulums as part of his mathematical studies. He knew that the science of

Watches were not uncommon by the late sixteenth century. Christian Huygens inserted a balance spring, regulating the motion. He presented the watch to Louis XIV.

astronomy needed accurate timekeeping, and he began designing a clock. In 1656, Huygens patented the world's first pendulum clock. It was the most accurate clock yet, off by less than a minute a day. Huygens built several pendulum clocks to determine longitude, and they were tried aboard ships at sea in 1662 and again in 1686. But the motion of the sea threw off the accuracy of his clocks. He described his findings in *Horologium Oscillatorium sive de Motu Pendulorum*, published in 1673. Huygens died in 1695.

Seventeenth-century clocks came to have various names, all depending on the look of their cases. There were birdcage clocks, lantern clocks, and sheep's-head clocks. Most of these cases were made of wood or brass. Most had bells or small gongs at the top to strike the hours. Colonists who immigrated to America, particularly to New England and Virginia, took such clocks with them, and they became common possessions as the colonies grew. About this time, clocks that had long cases were developed. These were made of wood and hid the long pendulums that kept them going. They were the ancestors of grandfather clocks. By the end of the seventeenth century, these long cases of wood were often beautifully inlaid or ornamented with brass or gold.

By 1671, a new type of escapement had been invented. It was called the anchor escapement because it hung like an anchor. It swung back and forth with the pendulum of the clock, with each swing either catching or releasing the clock's wheel. This regular action made

pendulum clocks even more dependable. They were able, for the first time, to count minutes and even seconds. One of those working with anchor escapement clocks was Robert Hooke, an architect, inventor, and scientist who lived from 1635 to 1703. Around 1657, he designed and patented the first anchor escapement clock, although whether or not Hooke actually invented the anchor escapement is not known.

Hooke's name is also linked to another aspect of time. An active intelligent scientist, he was also fascinated by fossils and geology. In the seventeenth century, no one was quite sure what fossils were. The problem was made worse by the fact that most people still believed that the earth was only a few thousand years old. Scientists intuitively suspected that this could not be so, but they had no explanation for what fossils were, and they were reluctant to challenge accepted church doctrine. Hooke was the first scientist to examine fossils with a microscope. As a result, he was able to see clear similarities between fossils and living shells, and petrified and living wood. He announced that the fossils

Above is Robert Hooke's compound microscope with illumination. The observations he made with it were recorded in Micrographia.

were definitely the remains of formerly living shellfish and trees. He was also one of the first scientists to realize that species can become extinct over time. But his ideas were not yet widely accepted. They seemed too strange to be true if the earth was really only a few thousand years old.

In the late seventeenth century, the measurement of longitude remained as much of a problem as it had been for the Portuguese in the early sixteenth century. For every fifteen degrees of longitude that a ship sailed west, the local time for that ship moved back an hour. For every fifteen degrees of longitude that a ship sailed east, its local time moved forward an hour. But if

sailors were to accurately calculate their location, they needed to measure their local time against the time at a specific reference point. The difference in time would reflect the distance east or west of the prime meridian. Unfortunately, the pendulum clocks of the era could not keep accurate time because of the rolling motions of a ship at sea. King Charles II of England founded the Royal Observatory in 1675 to find a solution to that problem, but for almost fifty years, no solution was found.

THE EIGHTEENTH CENTURY

Timekeeping methods continued to improve into the eighteenth century. George Graham, who was born about 1674, was a self-taught English astronomer and inventor. Raised by his brother after his father's death, Graham was apprenticed to a London clock maker, Henry Aske, and studied with him from 1688 to 1695. After this apprenticeship, Graham became talented in designing and building precise measuring instruments. He also taught himself astronomy and was even published in scholarly journals. About 1710, he designed a clockwork device that was a model of the earth, the sun, and the planets. The planets moved around the sun as time passed. Constructed for Charles Boyle, the fourth earl of Orrery, it became known as an orrery. Meanwhile, the designs that Graham created from 1715 to 1755 improved the pendulum clock's accuracy. Graham died in 1751.

John Harrison, an Englishman who was born in 1693, was a carpenter and self-taught clock maker. Harrison had first become intrigued with the idea of building a better timepiece when he was sick as a boy and his parents had put a clock on his pillow to amuse him. It was the old-fashioned sort that let him watch the works in action. Harrison built his first clock, made all of wood, in 1713. Then, in 1714, the British government offered a challenge. A prize of £20,000 was offered to anyone who could solve the longitude problem. But neither Harrison nor anyone else was ready to claim the prize—not yet.

From 1713 through the mid-1720s, John Harrison and his brother James designed clocks together. Their first success was a clock for a family named Pelham. What made this clock important was that it was the first to need no lubrication, or oiling. This was important because most clock oils of the era were notoriously bad, more likely to foul a clock's works than clean them. The brothers went on to design better and more accurate clocks than any other clock makers in London.

Harrison, however, remained interested in the British government's challenge. By 1761, he had invented a marine chronometer that could keep time on board a rolling ship to an accuracy of about one-fifth of a second a day. This won Harrison the prize. However, the Royal Observatory members hated the idea of giving the prize to a nonscientist and someone who didn't even have a college degree. They argued and stalled. It wasn't until 1773 and after years of bitter struggle that Harrison, who finally had to ask for the help of King George III, claimed his reward. Harrison died three years later, in 1776, possibly worn out by his struggle for recognition.

3

Improving the Accuracy of Timekeeping

In the nineteenth century, there was tremendous growth in industrialization, world trade, and scientific knowledge. People were beginning to realize that some global form of timekeeping was necessary. Perhaps the first in the United States to see the growing need for some type of

standardization of time measurements was an amateur astronomer named William Lambert. In 1809, he sent a recommendation to this effect to the United States Congress, but no one in government at that time was interested in taking up such a project.

Meanwhile, new questions about the actual age of the earth were being raised. Geology, the scientific study of the earth and its rocks and minerals, had started up in the eighteenth century with the basic goal of finding useful minerals for industry. But by the second half of the nineteenth century, the new science of geology had become more sophisticated. Geologists studying the earth raised the possibility that the processes that had shaped the earth had taken not thousands of years but millions and probably billions of years. Archbishop James Ussher had been finally proven wrong. The earth could not have been created in 4004 BC. It was a great deal older. The question that was bothering scientists now was how old was the earth?

James Ussher's chronology of Creation was widely disregarded by the 1800s. However, Creationists, who interpret the Bible very literally, still embrace Ussher's chronology.

GEOLOGIC TIME

Englishman Sir Charles Lyell was one of those interested in proving that the earth had evolved through incredibly long ages, what was beginning to be called geologic time. Born in 1797, the oldest of ten children, Lyell developed an early interest in geology, and it became his chosen career. He was deeply influenced by the work of an earlier Scottish geologist, James Hutton. In his three-volume work, *Principles of Geology,* published from 1860 to 1863, Lyell stated that common and well-understood geological processes,

still at work, were enough to explain the present form of the earth. He stated that a combination of the processes of volcanism (earthquakes and volcanic eruptions) and the processes of erosion (the actions of glaciers, water, and wind) was enough

Charles Lyell's Principles of Geology *was an influential geological work in the mid-1800s. Lyell was the first prominent scientist to promote Darwin's* Origin of Species.

to explain the geological features of our planet. At the time, this was known as the uniformitarian principle because it supported a slow and uniform series of changes that took place over great lengths of time. Given enough time, incremental changes could account for the dramatic geological formations one observed all over the earth.

This theory went against another viewpoint that was popular at the time, the theory of catastrophism. This idea suggested that the earth's geological features had been created suddenly in a series of rapid cataclysmic events, like floods and other major upheavals. Catastrophism did not require the earth to be very old, and this was the favored theory of theologians and conservative thinkers who believed that miracles and divine interventions had given the earth its present form. Lyell and his supporters advocated a vast timescale for the earth's history and stressed that the age of the human species also had to be far beyond the accepted theories of that time. Lyell died in 1875.

CHARLES DARWIN

Lyell's close friend was fellow Englishman Charles Darwin. Darwin, who was born in 1809, was to add a new element to the idea of geologic time through his theory of evolution. This theory stated that living organisms changed with the passage of time, mainly as a result of natural selection, the process by which creatures better adapted to their local environments would reproduce more effectively and survive. All creatures were related to each other through common ancestors in the past, but the creatures alive today looked different from their ancestors and each other because they had adapted to their environments. In his 1859 book *On the Origin of Species by Means of Natural Selection, or the Preservation of Favoured Races in the Struggle for Life*, known more simply as *The Origin of Species*, Darwin stated that most evolutionary change was gradual, requiring millions or billions of years. Many people were upset by the theory of

Best known for studying larger organisms, Charles Darwin also scrutinized those unseen by the human eye alone, using this microscope.

evolution. They refused to believe that human beings had evolved just like other animals or that humans and other primates were related. Darwin died in 1882. The controversy over evolution still continues, but evolution has been accepted by the scientific community and is now considered the fundamental principle of the biological sciences. In any case, Darwin's theory, like Lyell's, required an enormous span of time if incremental changes in the appearance of the earth and the creatures living on it were to take place.

LORD KELVIN'S THEORY

In addition to the objections by religious conservatives, there were scientific objections to Lyell's and Darwin's theories. The British physicist Lord Kelvin (1824–1907), who was the leading authority of the time on heat energy and thermodynamics, assumed that the earth had originally been molten. Knowing all about rates of cooling and heat transfer, he calculated that it had taken no more than 20 to 100 million years for the earth to cool to its

present temperature distribution. Though this was still an enormous span of time, it was not enough time for the processes of evolution to take place, and Kelvin's conclusions troubled Darwin. But Kelvin had assumed there was no source of "new" heat within the Earth. He was wrong.

Lord Kelvin's calculations of Earth's age were disregarded, but his credibility could not be denied after he invented a compass for use aboard ships and created the absolute temperature scale.

EXPANDING THE EARTH'S AGE

What Kelvin had not considered was the phenomenon of radioactivity. Scientists Pierre and Marie Curie

60

became famous for their research on the radiation given off by chemical elements such as uranium and thorium. British scientist Ernest Rutherford established the nuclear model of the atom and began to theorize about the transmutation of elements when they spontaneously gave off decay particles. The point was that the earth's interior was full of radioactive elements that gave off heat energy in the process of decay. As a result, the earth was not cooling as rapidly as Kelvin thought. It might very well be as old as proposed by Lyell and Darwin.

The first scientific attempts to calculate the age of the earth were based on how long it would take for the total thickness of the sedimentary rocks in the earth's crust to accumulate. Sedimentary rocks are those created from layer after layer of sand and other sediments that accumulate and are compressed by their weight into solid rocks, a process that was thought to occur at a uniform rate. But the strata (layers) of sedimentary rocks vary so greatly in their thickness from area to area that these investigations did not produce useful results. In 1899, an attempt to judge the age of the earth through the

salt in the oceans also failed, since salt from land that erodes into the sea is often recycled back into the land.

The work of Rutherford and other scientists on radioactivity, however, had led to the discovery that the rate of radioactive decay of each unstable element is regular. That regular rate of decay could be used, in a technique called radiometric dating, to determine the age of various rocks. In 1913, British geologist Arthur Holmes, who was working on his doctoral degree, proposed the first geological timescale based on the rates of radioactive decay. He made an estimate of the age of the earth that was far greater than anyone had suggested until then: 4 billion years. That was remarkably close to the age accepted by today's geologists, a little more than 4.5 billion years.

The result of all these investigations was that people were confronted with the idea of a span of time for the existence of living creatures, the earth, and the universe that was unimaginably long, so long that it seemed to render recorded human history almost insignificant by comparison.

IMPROVING THE ACCURACY OF TIMEKEEPING

ESTABLISHING STANDARD TIME

The accurate measurement of present time was also becoming more and more important. The age of industry required it. For example, how could anyone effectively run a railroad if people did not have an accurate idea of the time? How would anyone know when a train was going to leave one station or arrive at another? In 1830, the U.S. Navy established the Depot of Charts and Instruments, which was later to become the U.S. Naval Observatory. Its main mission was to care for the U.S. Navy's chronometers, charts, and other navigational equipment and to keep the chronometers calibrated for accuracy. It was the start of one of the agency's main jobs: timekeeping.

In the 1840s, a railway standard time for Great Britain—England, Scotland, and Wales—was developed to replace the separate "local time" systems. In 1845, in the city of Washington, D.C., the U.S. Naval Observatory, at the request of the secretary of the navy, installed what was called a time ball on top of the dome

of the observatory's telescope. Every day, precisely at noon, the time ball was dropped. This set the official time for people in Washington and for ships in the area that were setting out to sea. Thirty years later, a time ball atop the Western Union Building in New York City—then the tallest building in the city—was dropped by telegraphic signal from the Naval Observatory in Washington.

The Royal Observatory in Greenwich, England, began transmitting time telegraphically in 1852. By 1855, most of Britain was using what came to be known as Greenwich mean (or standard) time (GMT). A few clocks, like the large one on Tom Tower at Christ Church College, Oxford, were refitted with two hour hands, one for local time and one for GMT.

Greenwich became important for timekeeping in a different way as well. Until the second half of the nineteenth century, no two countries used the same "prime" meridian, or starting point, for determining longitude. The Greenwich meridian became the most popular prime meridian, partly because of the reliability

The bell in Tom Tower of Christ Church College still rings to mark the local time in Oxford, England—five minutes and two seconds behind GMT.

and correctness of the Greenwich Observatory's data and partly because the British Empire was so predominant around the world. In 1884, a conference was held in Washington, D.C. Forty-one delegates from twenty-five nations decided that the Greenwich meridian would be the prime meridian both for longitude and for keeping world time. The exact position of this meridian was marked by the position of the large Transit Circle telescope in the Greenwich Observatory's Meridian Building.

IMPROVING THE ACCURACY OF TIMEKEEPING

East and west of the Greenwich meridian, the world was divided into twenty-four time zones, matching the twenty-four hours in a day, though of course these zones can't be seen except on maps. However, in some countries, the borders of these zones aren't perfectly straight and follow national boundaries instead. In 1918, the United States government officially accepted Greenwich mean time and the Greenwich meridian as the standard timekeeping system, and the worldwide arrangement of time zones was accepted through an act of Congress.

As the United States grew and rail and telegraph lines were put in place, the Naval Observatory began its Time Service Department. This began just after the Civil War in 1865. A time signal was transmitted over telegraph lines to the Navy Department and activated the

One of the most important duties at the Royal Navy Observatory in Greenwich was the care and accurate rating of the nautical chronometers, which would be used on ships for navigation, most probably in wartime.

Washington fire bells at 7:00 AM, noon, and 6:00 PM. The service was sent across the nation via Western Union telegraph lines to give the railroads accurate time as well.

The railroad industry in the United States implemented the Standard Railway Time System in 1883. It was adopted by most—but not all—U.S. cities, and many people argued about it for years. The city of Detroit, Michigan, flatly refused to change from local time, which the city kept until 1900, when half of the city did switch to the standard system. The other half, though, still refused to change, and Detroit went back to its own local time. But in 1905, people gave up the fight, and Detroit joined the standard time of the rest of the country.

ADVANCEMENTS IN ACCURACY

In an experiment in 1880 that almost no one but scientists noticed, two Frenchmen, the brothers Pierre and Jacques Curie, discovered that if an electric field was applied to a quartz crystal, the crystal would vibrate. They called this effect piezoelectricity. For almost forty years, no one found a use for this effect, but it was going to play a large role in improved timekeeping in the modern age.

At the same time that standard time was being established, further innovations were producing better clocks. In 1889, a clock built by Siegmund Riefler had a nearly free pendulum that gave it an accuracy within a hundredth of a second a day. This clock became the standard in many astronomical observatories. Nine years later, R. J. Rudd introduced a true free-pendulum clock. After this, several companies designed free-pendulum clocks.

The most important of the free-pendulum clocks was the W. H. Shortt clock. It appeared in 1921 and almost immediately replaced the Riefler clock in the observatories. The Shortt clock contained two pendulums, called by the awkward names of slave and master. The "slave" pendulum gave the "master" pendulum soft pushes to keep it in motion and drove the clock's hands as well. This kept the "master" pendulum free to do nothing but move with regular precision.

But the Shortt clock was quickly overtaken by something new in time-keeping. In 1927, a Canadian engineer named Warren Marrison, working for Bell Laboratories in the United States, produced the first quartz clock. From the 1920s on, quartz clocks became more and more popular, since they offered much better performance than anything that had come before.

The world's first atomic clock had an error rate of one second every four months. By replacing ammonia molecules with cesium, the rate of error became one second every 2,000 years

Quartz is a common mineral that is found in many types of rocks. It is also one of the hardest minerals and doesn't erode easily. There are many varieties: everything from amethyst and rose quartz, which are used in

70

jewelry, to quartz sand and clear rock crystal. Quartz has many uses both in science and industry, and many of those are due to the piezoelectric effect that French scientists Pierre and Jacques Curie discovered in 1880. When a slice of quartz crystal is compressed, it develops a positive charge on one side and a negative charge on the other, like the positive and negative ends of a magnet. Electricity applied to a quartz crystal slice causes the slice to expand and contract, producing steady vibrations. Quartz crystal clocks have no gears or escapements to wear out and cause inaccuracies.

In 1945, Isidor Rabi, a Columbia University physics professor, suggested that an even more accurate clock could be developed using a technique called atomic beam magnetic resonance, which used the natural vibrations of atoms instead of quartz crystals. Rabi's method worked. In 1949, the National Bureau of Standards—now the National Institute of Standards and Technology—announced the world's first atomic clock, which used molecules of ammonia. It was less reliable than quartz clocks and was never used for timekeeping,

but it was a working prototype, a model from which to start working on more practical designs.

Improvements in electronic technology, meanwhile, allowed quartz clocks to be made smaller. By 1961, portable quartz clocks were being produced, and quartz crystals were—and still are—being used in most wristwatches. Today, quartz clocks and watches can be found everywhere because they provide very good performance for a low price. Through the 1960s, both the National Bureau of Standards in the United States and the National Physical Laboratory in England worked on developing more and more advanced atomic clocks, using the element cesium.

The container of an atomic clock holds a microwave radio transmitter, which gives off a steady series of high-frequency radio waves, like a miniature radar set. When the radio waves hit the cesium atoms, the atoms absorb them and in the process give off light. A photocell, which is like the electric eye sensor in a modern door, tracks the light. Whenever the light gets dimmer, the photocell sends a signal to the radio transmitter, which adjusts its frequency. A counter reads the radio waves generated by the transmitter. A computer translates the numbers from the counter into a readable signal that looks like the reading from a digital clock.

By 1964, atomic clocks had reached an accuracy of within one second in 6,000 years. Since cesium atoms were proving themselves so dependable, the cesium atom's natural frequency, or rate of vibration, was accepted in 1967 as the new international unit of time. A second was defined as exactly 9,192,631,770 oscillations, or "ticks," of the cesium atom. In 1972, coordinated universal time (UTC) was adopted as the official time for the world. The Bureau International des Poids et Mesures, or International Bureau of Weights and Measures, in Paris acts as the official time-keeper of atomic time for the world. Sixty-five laboratories around the world with 230 atomic clocks are used to calculate this complex measurement.

Atomic clock design is still being refined. By the 1990s, atomic clocks were accurate to within one

second in six million years. By 2002, atomic clocks were capable of keeping time to about 30 billionths of a second per year. It's almost impossible to imagine a clock's accuracy being off by such an incredibly tiny figure. And some people may wonder why such a precise clock is necessary.

One use of precise timing is in the pinpointing of locations. The Global Positioning System, or GPS, is a network of satellites, each carrying three atomic clocks. A GPS unit on the ground, in the air, or at sea receives radio signals from at least four of these satellites and can accurately calculate its location. In addition to being used by the U.S. Department of Defense, GPS is also used by commercial companies, police and fire departments, scientists tracking endangered animals, and even by individual hikers. What's more, during construction of the tunnel under the English Channel, British and French crews started digging from opposite ends and used GPS receivers to make sure they met up perfectly in the middle. Telephone companies also use atomic clocks to make sure that long-distance data exchanges are coordinated.

A biologist monitors his GPS unit while walking through the Imperial Sand Dunes in El Centro, California. This ability to accurately calculate time and position even helps with knowledge of how to protect the earth's endangered species.

DAYLIGHT SAVING TIME

Daylight saving time is a system in which clocks are set one hour forward at a certain date in the spring to allow one more hour of daylight and, technically, to save electricity by reducing evening use of lights by an hour. The clocks are then set back one hour at a certain date in

the autumn. In the United States, daylight saving time always begins on the first Sunday in April and ends on the last Sunday in October. Not all states follow daylight saving time. Arizona, Hawaii, and Indiana do not.

Some countries went to daylight saving time during a time of war, when energy needed to be conserved. Both Britain and the United States adopted such a plan during World War I (1914–1918) and again during World War II (1939–1945). But after 1945, many countries kept daylight saving time. In the United States, the official policy began in 1967, although it wasn't until 1987 that daylight saving time began on the first Sunday in April. In Europe, the daylight saving period is called the summer time period. It begins a week earlier than in the United States, but it ends at the same time.

TIME ZONES

Because of its size, there are four time zones in the continental United States—eastern, central, mountain, and Pacific. When it is 12 PM in the eastern standard time (EST) zone, it is 11 AM in the central standard time (CST) zone, 10 AM in the mountain standard time (MST) zone, and 9 AM in the Pacific standard time (PST) zone. Because of its distance from the rest of the country, Alaska's time is an hour behind Pacific standard time, and Hawaii's time is two hours behind Pacific standard time.

Of all the large nations, only China does not use time zones. Because the whole country has only the one standard time, when it is light at noon in eastern China, it can be dark at noon in western China, since the sun hasn't risen there yet.

Modern Concepts of Time

4

In the twenty-first century, we recognize many different concepts of time. In physics, time is one of the fundamental properties of the universe, like length and mass and electric charge. Material objects not only have mass and spatial dimensions, but they exist at or for certain

Can we look back in time? Some astronomers are turning their telescopes in the direction from which the universe is expanding and seeing remnants of the big bang.

lengths of time, and in the most advanced studies of the cosmos, time is considered another dimension. In fact, it cannot be considered separately from the other dimensions, and physicists speak of the conjoined phenomena space-time. It is known that the universe is expanding, so space and time appear to move

together. Time, it should be noted, moves only in one direction, forward, never backward, a consequence of the laws of thermodynamics, which state that heat energy can move only in one direction, from higher to lower temperatures.

EXAMINING TIME'S ARROW

The forward flow of time is sometimes called time's arrow, and it is determined by the thermodynamic principle of entropy, or increasing disorder. If the universe continues to expand, scientists have to consider the possibility that eventually all the potential heat energy stored in matter will be evenly distributed throughout the universe. That energy will then be "unavailable," that is, it can no longer be made to flow from one place to another because there will be no temperature differentials anywhere in the cosmos. Physical processes caused by the transfer of heat energy will cease, and this is called the "heat death" of the universe.

MODERN CONCEPTS OF TIME

Scientists have always wondered, and continue to wonder, about the origin of the universe, including the origin of time. How did time begin? The question has been answered with a theory known as the big bang model of the universe. The theory states that about 12 to 14 billion years ago, all the matter in the entire universe was crammed into an unimaginably small space. A sudden powerful explosion occurred, and the hot, dense mass of the universe-to-be was thrown apart, expanding outward in all directions. Time began with that primordial explosion and continued as the new universe began to evolve into stars, planets, and everything else.

Did time exist before the big bang? This is a problematic question for scientists because they work only with measurable quantities. Time can be measured by the rate or speed at which objects change position or the way that events succeed each other. As the universe expands and the distances between objects change at measurable rates, we can comprehend the notion of time. Before the universe existed, before there was any

space in which objects could move, the notion of time is difficult to define.

THE THEORIES OF ALBERT EINSTEIN

In the first decades of the twentieth century, the way scientists looked at time and space was changed forever. The reason for such a major change was the appearance of two theories, the special and the general theories of relativity, both created by the scientist Albert Einstein. Born in Germany in 1879, he was the most important physicist of the twentieth century and certainly one of the greatest and most famous scientists of all time.

In 1900, after his graduation from a university in Zurich, Switzerland, Einstein spent two years looking for

Einstein is pictured here circa 1905, often considered his "miracle year." His papers on his special theory of relativity and quantum theory were beginning to gain acceptance in the scientific community.

work. He finally settled for a job at the patent office in Bern, Switzerland, where he worked from 1902 to 1909, reviewing patent applications for new inventions. This was a routine job, not one that needed much attention for someone as sharp as Einstein was, and it allowed him a great deal of free time for thinking about physics.

Einstein was struck by an idea, which he wrote up in 1905 as the special theory of relativity. In it, he stated, among other things, that time is not absolute. What this means is that the measurement of time depends on where someone is and how fast that person is moving in relation to the objects he or she is observing. Only the speed of light, Einstein wrote, is always the same. For the speed of light to remain constant for all observers, both distance and time would have to change to keep everything balanced. Einstein showed that how fast time moves depends on how fast the clock measuring that time is moving. The faster the clock is being physically moved, the more slowly time passes for that clock, as measured by an observer who is not moving with that clock. Astronauts traveling out into space and back to the earth on a very fast spaceship, one able to move close to the speed of light, would find themselves faced with an odd problem. They might have spent only five years in space, from their point of view, but on the earth, about thirty years might have passed. While in their swift ship, the passage of time would appear to pass at the same rate, but when they returned to the earth, they would not have aged as much as those they left behind.

Einstein also showed that the faster an object went, the more mass it acquired—the more resistant it became to further changes in its motion—and therefore the more energy it needed to be pushed even faster. To go faster than the speed of light was impossible, since it would take an infinite amount of energy to push an infinitely massive object.

In 1906, Einstein's former college teacher in mathematics, Hermann Minkowski, came up with a new idea for considering space and time. Space and time were

to be combined into a new physical entity called space-time. The mathematics of relativity revealed that space and time had to be combined if the equations are to accurately describe what we see. Because space has three dimensions—height, width, and depth—and time has one dimension, our universe has to be, at a minimum, four-dimensional. Scientists now consider our world and everything around it to be part of a four-dimensional space-time continuum (a sequence or progression).

What does it mean to say that an object has a certain number of dimensions? It means that it takes a certain number of coordinates, or numbers, to describe the physical properties of that object. To locate an object in space, using any other point as a reference, we need to specify three numbers, equivalent to length, width, and depth. But because objects are in motion, we also have to specify a fourth number, representing when the object exists.

In a research paper published in 1916, Einstein, with his general theory of relativity, showed that gravity

Albert Einstein won the Nobel Prize for Physics in 1921 for his work on the photoelectric effect. He described how light had a particle effect as well as a wave effect. When these particles hit atoms of certain substances, electrons were emitted.

could bend light. His claim was proved three years later during a 1919 solar eclipse, when British astronomer Arthur S. Eddington detected the bending of starlight by the sun's enormous gravitational field. Einstein also showed that gravity could affect time. The gravitational field of a massive object like the earth should cause

clocks closer to the object to appear to run slower, just as if they were accelerating to high velocities.

In 1962, two atomic clocks that scientists mounted at the top and bottom of a water tower provided a chance to test Einstein's theory about time and gravity. Sure enough, Einstein was right. The clock at the bottom of the tower, closer to the center of the earth's mass, did appear to run more slowly than the clock at the top of the tower. Many other experiments have since demonstrated the correctness of Einstein's theory. Scientists have measured the rates of decay of subatomic particles entering the earth's atmosphere as cosmic rays at speeds close to the speed of light. These particles appear to take longer to decay, or transform themselves into other particles, than in laboratory experiments where the particles are not moving so fast.

Sir Arthur Eddington, British astronomer and admired contemporary of Einstein's, is considered the father of modern theoretical astrophysics. After proving Einstein's theory of relativity, he turned his focus to studying the internal makeup of stars.

BLACK HOLES

The equations of Einstein's general theory also predict the existence of what scientists call black holes. If gravity can bend light, it is conceivable that the region of space surrounding a very massive object would experience a gravitational force so strong that light rays bend completely around the object and no light can escape from that region. The distance from such a massive object where light turns on itself is called the event horizon. Within this horizon, we see nothing and can obtain no information about what is happening. At the event horizon, to distant observers, time slows to a standstill. A black hole can form when a massive star runs out of its nuclear fuel and its core collapses in on itself, crushed by its own gravitational force. If the star's core has enough mass, the collapse continues until all that mass is concentrated at a tiny point in its center, possibly smaller than the nucleus of an atom. Physicists call this point a singularity. Within that singularity, we have no conception of what is happening to the material objects trapped there. All we know is that the mass is still there, because of the continuing presence of a powerful gravitational field.

Though no light escapes from inside the event horizon, black holes are not entirely invisible. Just outside the event horizon, the matter falling inward is subjected to such tremendous forces that it begins to give off intense radiation. There are thought to be many black holes throughout our galaxy, and one of the ways we try to detect them is by looking in the sky for regions of space that give off large numbers of gamma rays or X-rays. These spots of intense radiation indicate that powerful forces are at work in these regions, though we may detect no objects like stars there.

TIME TRAVEL

But if time can be slowed down, can it also run backward? Is time travel to the past really possible? Time travel was an established part of science fiction even before Einstein proposed his theories. British author H. G. Wells wrote his

famous novel *The Time Machine* in 1895. But modern scientists are very skeptical of such an idea. As mentioned, the known laws of thermodynamics require that the energy in a closed system flow in one direction only. If objects or people could remove themselves from one time frame and move to another,

Herbert George Wells, pictured here in 1920, is known for such works as The War of the Worlds. *He often used his science fiction writings as social commentary.*

all sorts of contradictions would arise between the causes of events and their effects. That would mean abandoning most of the principles of modern science. And where could one go in the past? The universe is in motion, and the earth and the stars and the galaxies no longer exist in the space-time where they existed yesterday. Could the

The movie The Time Machine *(1960) was based on Wells's 1895 novel. Wells was ahead of his time in describing a machine that treated time as a fourth dimension. This was years before Einstein's theory of a four-dimensional space-time continuum.*

whole cosmos be rewound as if it were a motion picture film or a videotape? Movement in time appears to be different from linear movement through the other dimensions, and explaining how it might occur requires enormous complications to known science that have little experimental justification. And yet . . .

HOW DO WE KNOW
The Nature of Time

In the 1980s, astronomer Carl Sagan (1934–1996) was working on a science fiction novel. For purposes of the plot, he wanted his characters to be able to use a shortcut through space by traveling from earth through a black hole to a distant world. This wouldn't be possible by the accepted rules of physics, particularly since the intense gravity within a black hole would crush anything even getting near it. So Dr. Sagan asked a fellow scientist and friend, theoretical physicist Kip S. Thorne, for advice. Working at the California Institute of Technology, Professor Thorne carries out research on black holes and the nature of space, time, and gravity.

Einstein had pondered the idea of a wormhole as early as 1913. Now Thorne would refine it. A wormhole was thought to be a kind of tunnel through space-time created by a black hole, linking distant

Astronomer Carl Sagan, pictured here in 1974, advised NASA on several unmanned missions. He designed a plaque for Pioneer 10 *(upper left), launched in 1972, in case it encountered intelligent life. The last signal from the decaying space probe was received on January 23, 2003.*

parts of the universe. Matter would fall in, but instead of being crushed into a singularity, it would somehow be transported to a different region of space. Sagan finished his novel, *Contact*, in 1985, and it was made into a movie in 1997. Later, Thorne speculated that a wormhole could also be used to travel backward in time. A wormhole that takes a shortcut through space-time could just as easily link two different times as two different places. Professor Thorne has been studying the subject of wormholes ever since. His book on the subject, *Black Holes and Time Warps: Einstein's Outrageous Legacy*, was published in 1995.

Are there such wormholes anywhere in the space-time continuum? It is pure speculation that such phenomena exist. Mathematical equations say that wormholes are at least possible. Can we use them to travel across space or through time? Right now, the answer is apparently not. According to the equations, if wormholes really do exist, they would be too small and unstable for any safe use. It looks as though travel through wormholes is something for science fiction.

MODERN CONCEPTS OF TIME

The laws of causality make some people argue that time travel simply won't work. They mention the "grandfather paradox" as a case in point. In this scenario, you go back in time, and for whatever reason, you kill your grandfather. But when you kill him, you end your family history and cease to exist. You therefore aren't around to go back to kill your grandfather. Resolving such conundrums seems impossible if time travel can actually occur.

There's another interesting argument from those who think time travel is impossible. They say that if time travel is possible, we should already have met time travelers from the future. In fact, our entire world should already have been turned upside down by the interference and changes caused by visitors from the future. But if that were true, would we know it? With each change to the past, history would be rewritten, along with our memories and experiences. We would wake up each day, so to speak, with no knowledge that we had lived differently yesterday. In that case, our memories are illusory. One can begin to see the enormous difficulties in the recording and measurement of the physical

Here, the earth is seen as an atom. Today, some physicists are eager to prove a theory that would link the smallest particle of matter to the universe as a whole. Superstring theory describes the point at which no particle can be divided further. What is left is a vibrating string, which is the universe's common thread.

world, in our faith in the continuity of our experiences, and in the foundations of science as we understand them, if time travel were possible. This makes it very distasteful to most scientists.

On the level of the quantum, however, the microscopic level at which we examine the behavior of subatomic particles, some experiments have been conducted whose results seem to imply that the laws of causality can be violated. These subtle experiments seem to be telling us that under some circumstances, information can be transmitted faster than the speed of light or a single subatomic particle can exist in two places at once. And some theoretical calculations have led to the concept of the tachyon, a particle that cannot move slower than the speed of light and that moves backward in time as soon as it is created. But such experiments and calculations are on the very cutting edge of physics, and we are not at all sure what their results mean or what they are telling us about the physical world. One thing is abundantly clear—we don't know everything yet!

Glossary

atomic clock An extremely precise timekeeping device based on the natural vibrations of cesium atoms or other chemical elements.

big bang A theory of the start of the universe, which states that all matter was compressed into a tiny point billions of years ago and then expanded.

black hole An extremely small region of space-time, possibly a collapsed massive star, with a gravitational field from which nothing can escape.

calendar A device for keeping track of days, weeks, months, and years.

daylight saving time A system that adds an hour of daylight in the summer by moving clocks forward an hour in the spring and back an hour in the autumn.

Greenwich mean time The standard time on which the world's time is based, also called universal time.

latitude The imaginary lines running east to west, dividing up the globe in horizontal segments.

longitude The imaginary lines running north to south on the globe that are the important dividers of local times.

space-time continuum The universe and everything in it, in which time and space are joined.

theory A scientific idea or concept based on as much fact as possible and devised to explain the nature or behavior of something.

time machine In fiction, a machine that lets someone travel backward or forward in time.

for More Information

The Franklin Institute
222 North 20th Street
Philadelphia, PA 19103
(215) 448-1200
Web site: http://sln.fi.edu

Liberty Science Center
Liberty State Park
251 Phillips Street
Jersey City, NJ 07305
Web site: http://www.lsc.org

Museum of Science
Science Park
Boston, MA 02114
Web site: http://www.mos.org

**National Institute of Standards
and Technology**
325 Broadway, Mailcode 847.00
Boulder, CO 80305-3328
Web site: http://www.bldrdoc.gov/timefreq/
index.html

**The Nelson-Atkins Museum
of Art**
4525 Oak Street
Kansas City, MO 64111-1873
(816) 561-4000
Web site: http://www.nelson-atkins.org/tempusfugit/
default2.htm

**Exploratorium at the Palace
  of Fine Arts**
3601 Lyon Street
San Francisco, CA 94123
(415) 561-0399
Web site: http://www.exploratorium.edu

WEB SITES

Due to the changing nature of Internet links, the Rosen Publishing Group, Inc., has developed an online list of Web sites related to the subject of this book. This site is updated regularly. Please use this link to access the list:

http://www.rosenlinks.com/gsq/nati

for further Reading

Aust, Sigfried. *Clocks! How Time Flies.* Minneapolis: Lerner Publications, 1992.

Morris, Richard. *Time's Arrows.* New York: Simon & Schuster, 1985.

Pollard, Michael. *The Clock and How It Changed the World.* New York: Facts on File, 1995.

Shallis, Michael. *On Time.* New York: Schocken Books, 1983.

Zubrowski, Bernie. *Clocks: Building and Experimenting.* New York: William Morrow, 1988.

Bibliography

Andrewes, William J. H., ed. *The Quest for Longitude.* Cambridge, MA: Harvard University, 1996.

Audoin, Claude, and Bernard Guinot. *The Measurement of Time: Time, Frequency, and the Atomic Clock.* Cambridge, UK: Cambridge University Press, 2001.

Bartky, Ian R. "The Adoption of Standard Time." *Technology and Culture*, Vol. 30, January 1989, pp. 25–56.

Dohrn-Van Rossum, Gerhard. *History of the Hour: Clocks and Modern Temporal Orders.* Chicago: University of Chicago Press, 1998.

Howse, Derek. *Greenwich Time and the Discovery of the Longitude.* London: Philip Wilson Publishers, Ltd., 1997.

Itano, Wayne M., and Norman F. Ramsey. "Accurate Measurement of Time." *Scientific American,* Vol. 269, July 1993, pp. 56–65.

Jespersen, James, and Jane Fitz-Randolph. *From Sundials to Atomic Clocks: Understanding Time and Frequency.* Mineola, NY: Dover Publications, 1999.

Jones, Tony. *Splitting the Second.* Bristol, UK: Institute of Physics Publishing, 2000.

Landes, Davis S. *A Revolution in Time: Clocks and the Making of the Modern World.* Cambridge, MA: Harvard University Press, 1985.

Morris, Richard. *Time's Arrows.* New York: Simon & Schuster, 1985.

Needham, Joseph, Wang Ling, and Derek J. deSolla Price. *Heavenly Clockwork: The Great Astronomical Clocks of Medieval China.* Cambridge, UK: Cambridge University Press, 1986.

Shallis, Michael. *On Time.* New York: Schocken
    Books, 1983.
Sobel, Dava. *Longitude.* New York: Penguin Books, 1995.
Thorne, Kip S. *Black Holes and Time Warps: Einstein's
    Outrageous Legacy.* New York: W. W. Norton &
    Company, 1995.

Index

Credits

ABOUT THE AUTHOR

Josepha Sherman is a professional author and folklorist, with more than forty books and 125 stories and articles in print. She's an active member of the Author's Guild and the Science Fiction Writers of America. Her Web site is at http://www.josephasherman.com.

Designer: Evelyn Horovicz; **Editor:** Leigh Ann Cobb;
Photo Researcher: Nelson Sá